Write from Start 3

Lynn Michell

Oliver & Boyd

Illustrated by:
Pat Tourret, Shirley Tourret, David Simmonds,
Lesley Smith, Joanna Williams, Tony Morris,
Michael Charlton,
Linda Birch and Lyn Vesco.

Oliver & Boyd
Robert Stevenson House
1–3 Baxter's Place
Leith Walk
Edinburgh EH1 3BB

A Division of Longman Group UK Ltd

First published 1987

ISBN 0 05 003946 6

Set in 14 on 18pt Helvetica

Produced by Longman Group (FE) Limited
Printed in Hong Kong

Contents

Teacher's Note

Write from the Start is a series of six books for children between the ages of six and twelve. It is designed to encourage children's awareness of the different purposes of writing and to develop their ability to use and apply its different forms for a variety of audiences.

The series covers both the expressive and the functional aspects of writing: stories; word play leading to poetry; speech bubbles leading to writing plays; messages of various kinds; instructions and information both given and received.

Book 2 develops and extends the work of the introductory level (Book 1) and invites the child to go beyond the activities given on the page. In Books 3 and 4 the framework and starting points for the writing tasks remain but there is more scope for children to draw on their own ideas and experiences as they write for different purposes and audiences. In Books 5 and 6 these props are gradually withdrawn and the varied writing tasks make considerable demands on children's abilities to think, plan and write appropriate texts.

It is not recommended that children be left to work through the books in isolation. There are ample opportunities for discussion and role-play (especially in the 'Voices' units) and teachers should feel free to extend and adapt all of the suggestions offered here. Indeed, without discussion and teacher participation, the effectiveness of this material will be reduced.

Teachers should also be selective and adaptable in the order in which they use the various units. We have offered an arrangement which makes logical sense and represents a progression within each unit. Other users may well have different ideas, though, and they should use these materials as a flexible resource rather than a strait-jacket. Teachers can take what they want at the time that suits them best. The important thing is to cover all these varieties of writing at some time during the school year.

The series does not set out to teach all aspects of English; it concerns itself with developing children's concepts of themselves as writers, their awareness of different writing styles and the various purposes to which writing skills need to be applied.

1 Voices

Everyday Conversations

We can use speech bubbles to show what people are saying.
Look at the pictures below.
What are the people saying to each other?

Try to think of a short conversation that sounds real.
Perhaps you could try it out with a friend.

Write a few words for each person in each picture.
Draw a speech bubble around each.
We have done the first one for you.

Comic Strips

In comic strips the words people speak
are written in speech bubbles.
Only the words actually spoken go inside the bubbles.

Here is the beginning of a picture story.
What do you think the people are saying in the third picture?

Here's part of another story.
What do you think the people are saying?

Write the words each person says.
Draw a speech bubble around each one.

Night Flight

Look at the pictures.
They tell the story of a boy who flies
to a magic land of birds.

What is the boy saying?
What are the birds saying?

Make up the words spoken.
Follow the numbers in the bubbles.

Write them like this.

1. Time to turn your light off now.

Then **draw** a picture showing how the story ends.
Include some spoken words.
Draw a bubble around the words.

Telephone Conversations

The phone rings.   Cathy answers it.

Who is it?
Why are they phoning?
Here are some suggestions. You can think of others.

- It is Cathy's friend. She wants to invite Cathy to a party.
- It is Cathy's Gran. She has just collected her new puppy. She wants to know if Cathy would like to go round.

You may be able to act out one of these conversations with a friend.

Write a short telephone conversation between yourself and another person. You can use one of the ideas above — or make up your own.
Start a new line each time one of you begins to speak.
Write the speaker's name at the side.
We have begun one conversation for you. You could try acting it out.

PETER	Hello
GRAN	Hello. It's me. Gran.
PETER	Hello, Gran.
GRAN	Peter, I've got the puppy!

(What else do they say?)

This time YOU make a phone call.
You are not at home and need to use
a phone box.
Here are some possible reasons.
Try acting one of them.
Decide who you are phoning and why.
You can use an idea from one
of the circles or make up your own.

Write a short telephone conversation
exactly as you did before.
Remember to start a new line
each time a new person begins to speak.

Perhaps your little brother has got
his head stuck in some railings.
You need to phone for help.

Perhaps you have won a giant
teddy in a toy
shop lucky dip.
He's too big
for you to
carry home.

Perhaps you have spotted the
flamingo reported missing on the
news. You must phone the zoo.

Perhaps you have met a friend in the
park and want to ask if she can come
home with you to tea.

Or is there a quite
different reason?

Here is a picture conversation.

JOANNA   Excuse me. Is this the way to the zoo?

MRS LEE   Yes. It's about two miles further along this road. Just keep going. You can't miss it.

Write a short conversation for each of these pictures.
It can be just two lines.
Give each person a name.
What are they saying to each other?

A

B

C
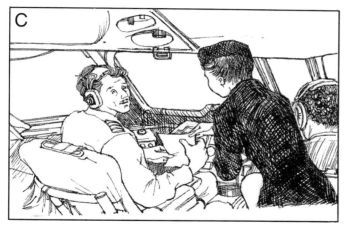

D

On the Bus

All the people in the pictures below are on a bus.
What are they saying to each other?
Give each person a name.
Make up their conversations.
You might try them out first with a friend.

Write at least two lines of conversation for each of the pictures,
as you did before.

When you have finished them all,
choose one picture and think of a **different** conversation
for the **same** two people.

A Longer Chat

Look at the first picture.
Mrs Brown and Julie are having quite a long chat.

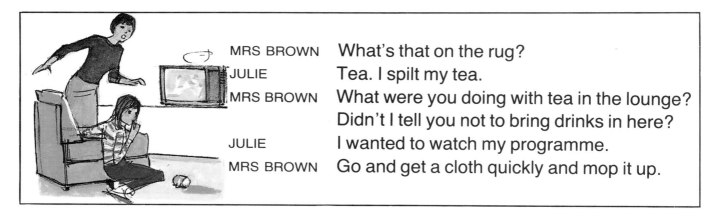

MRS BROWN	What's that on the rug?
JULIE	Tea. I spilt my tea.
MRS BROWN	What were you doing with tea in the lounge? Didn't I tell you not to bring drinks in here?
JULIE	I wanted to watch my programme.
MRS BROWN	Go and get a cloth quickly and mop it up.

Choose one of these three pictures.
Decide on names for two of the people.

Write a short conversation for the two people.
Try to make the conversation sound as real as possible.

Perhaps your teacher will let two of you act the conversation
in front of the class.

A

B

C

This is Sandy.

This is Craig.

They are good friends.
You can make Craig and Sandy puppets.

Draw and colour the two children on paper.
Stick the paper to card.
Carefully cut around the card.
(Remember to leave a long tab.)
Make up a short conversation for Craig and Sandy.
Choose one of the suggestions below.
Or make up a different conversation if you want.

- Talking about starting a new gang.
  Craig and Sandy will be leaders.
- Deciding what to buy with £5 which one of them
  won in a competition.
- Planning a birthday surprise for an old person
  they know in their street.

Write out the conversation between Craig and Sandy.
Perhaps your teacher will let two of you perform
your puppet conversation in front of the class.

2 Word Play

Adventure Playground

Words for movement

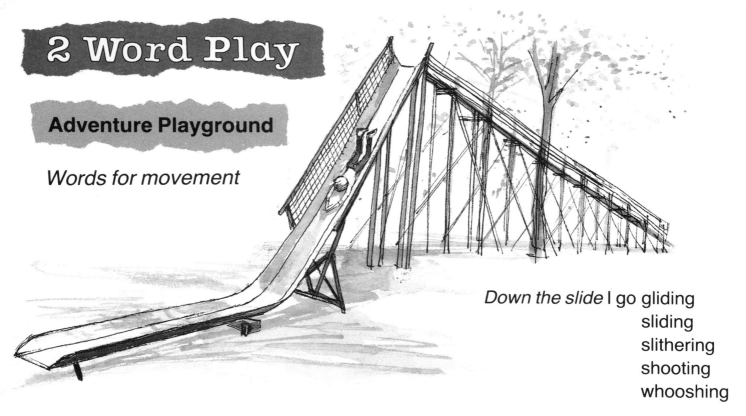

Down the slide I go gliding
sliding
slithering
shooting
whooshing

What is it like to play on the other things in the adventure playground?

Write some words to describe what it is like in the other pictures.
There are more on the next page.
You might use some words for more than one picture.

On the rope I go flying
?
?
?
?

On the death slide I go spinning
?
?
?
?

Up the web I go scrambling
?
?
?
?

Down the pole I go slipping
?
?
?
?

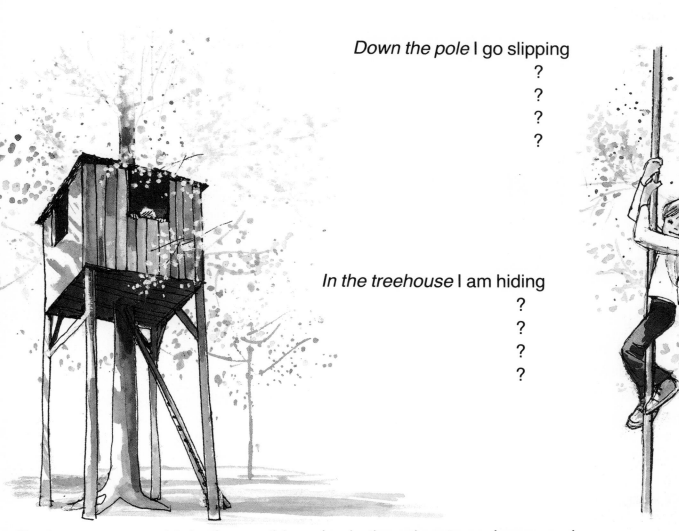

In the treehouse I am hiding
?
?
?
?

Perhaps you can think of something else in the adventure playground.
Write some words about it.

A LOUD Poem!

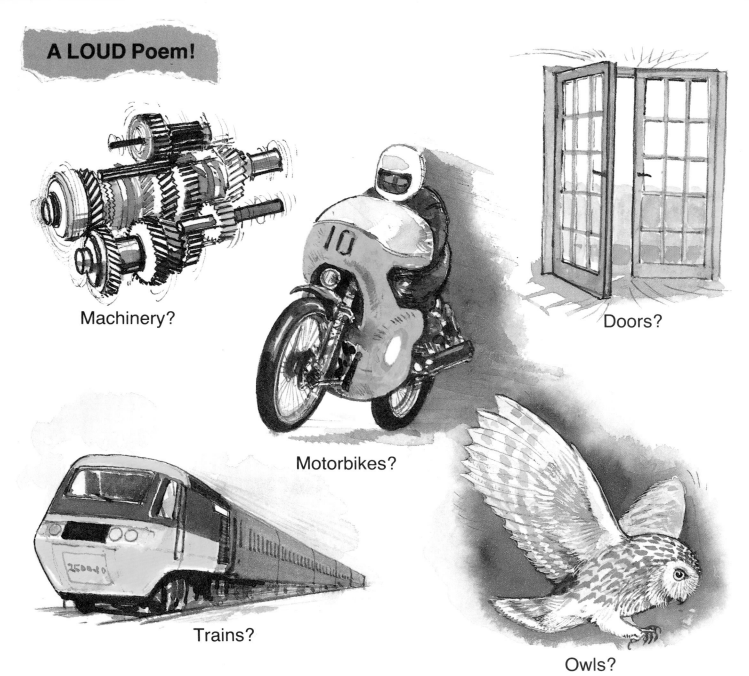

Machinery?

Doors?

Motorbikes?

Trains?

Owls?

Make up a LOUD poem.
Use our ideas and others of your own.
Make each line include one noisy thing and the noise it makes.
Write it like this

Motorbikes ROAR
Trains SCREAM

(and so on).

What else makes a LOUD noise?
Write your own LOUD poem.

Mice?

Grasses?

Ghosts?

Water?

Cats?

Write a QUIET poem.
Like this

Cats *purr*

(and so on).

What else makes a gentle, soft sound?
Think of lots more ideas of your own.
Write your own quiet poem.

Spells

When Hocus the Witch wants to make a spell for a new car she says:

> Claw and feather
> Bat and **fly**
> Make me a car
> That soars through the **sky**.

The words **fly** and **sky** rhyme.

Write a four-line spell like that one.
Make lines 2 and 4 rhyme.
Choose **one** of the following:

- a spell to bring on a thunderstorm,
- a spell to turn your worst enemy into a creature (you say which),
- a spell to close school tomorrow,
- a spell to make someone miserable smile,
- or something else. You decide.

Write out your spell neatly and add a picture of your own.

Magic and Mystery

Have you noticed how quite ordinary things can seem strange at night,
like a shadow, or shapes on the window?
Words can change ordinary things too.
Words can make things mysterious or frightening.

Like this   Ordinary by day   Strange at night

a raven   a black, swooping raven

Write your own extra words for these.
Choose words to make each thing seem mysterious.
Add two new ideas of your own.

Ordinary by day   Strange by night

a rat   a———rat   a shadow   a———shadow

a storm   a———storm   a shape   a———shape
                                 on a window   on a window

Mysterious Places

Where would you most expect something mysterious to happen?
Where would magic work best?

Look at the pictures on these two pages.
Which one would you choose as a place
for magic spells and scary happenings?

Write a short description of **one** of the places
— or a poem if you prefer.
You can use some of the ideas on the previous page if you want.
Make your place sound as secret and mysterious as possible.

Attic

Jungle

Wasteland

Ruins

3 Stories

People in Stories

What do they look like?
We like to know what people in stories look like.
Then we can 'see' them in our imagination.

This is Terry.
He is football-mad
    quick
    fit
    red-faced
    skinny
    muddy

Here are some more people.
Choose **two** of them.

Write a list of words like we did.
Describe what they look like.
Give each of your people a name.

What kind of people are they?

We like to know all about people in stories—

- how they behave,
- what they do,
- what they think about.

We like to know what kind of people they are.

This is Mick.

He is our gang-leader.
He is tough.
Sometimes he can be cruel.
He is afraid of nothing.
He wants a motor-bike.

Here are some more people.
Choose **two** and give them names.
What do you think they are like?

Write some things about them,
as we have done.

Someone I Know Well

Think of someone you know well.
Perhaps it is someone in your family or a friend.

- What do they look like?
- What do they like to do?
- What are they like?

This is what one child wrote about a special person.

David

This is my friend David. He is tall for his age. He has straight black hair cut short at the back. His mum likes it like that. He wears a duffle-coat to school even when it is hot. David is clever. He is keen on Adventure Game-Books. He carries his books and maps and notes around in a bright yellow bag. We laugh at him when he gets too serious and he sulks.

Write a short description of your person.
Tell us what they look like.
Tell us something about them.
What is special about them?
Draw a picture.

Favourite Character Posters

People in stories are called **characters**.
Do you have a favourite character —
someone in a story or film you specially like?
Is there one character who seems very real to you?
Perhaps it is an animal or a creature.
Think about the stories you have read and heard
and decide who is **your** favourite character.

Make a Favourite Character Poster.

1. **Draw and colour** a picture of your favourite character
    on a sheet of white paper.

2. **Write** something about the character—

    📕 who they are,
    📕 which story they are from,
    📕 what they look like,
    📕 what kind of person or animal they are,
    📕 why you like them.

3. **Cut out** your picture.
    Cut out your piece of writing.
    Arrange both on a larger sheet of coloured paper.

4. **Glue** them on the sheet of coloured paper.

Picture Stories

CATHY HAS DROPPED HER NEW BOX OF PICTURE CARDS. NOW SHE WILL HAVE TO SORT THEM OUT.

Cathy can't sort out two sets of cards.
Can you help her?

Write the correct order for each set of cards.
Begin like this—1, B, C, ? ?

THANK YOU FOR HELPING ME.
HERE ARE MORE OF MY PICTURES.

Write
The pictures below are now in the right order.
Choose one set of pictures and write a short story about them.

Story Consequences

Look and read

Here are the beginnings of three different stories.
Choose one and imagine what happens next.
Write a short story with Cathy's beginning, your middle and your end.

Mandy picked up the letter which the postman had brought.
It was addressed to her!
She opened the envelope and began to read . . . .

Frankie decided to take a short cut home down Preston Street.
No one lived there now.
The doors and windows were broken or boarded up.
Suddenly Rusty stopped and began to bark: . . . .

It was Wednesday — the day Emma went to the swimming baths
after school.
She changed quickly and dived into the water.
She thought she saw something on the bottom of the pool . . . .

Beginnings, Middles and Ends

Look and read

THIS TIME I'VE TAKEN THE MIDDLE CARD FROM SOME OF MY SETS OF PICTURES. CAN YOU THINK OF A BEGINNING AND AN END?

Choose one of the pictures below.
What do you think is happening in the picture?
Imagine what happened before.
Imagine what happens afterwards.

Write a short story with your beginning,
Cathy's middle and your ending.

Tom's Special Place

My treehouse is high in the old apple tree at the bottom of the garden. Some times no body knows I'm there. Inside there is a sleepingbag, some comics and a bag of apples in case it rains. If it is fine I can sit out on the branch and watch what's happening in the street below. Only my friend is allowed in the treehouse with me. We crawl inside and plan our adventures.

A Place I Know

You are going to write about a place you know very well.
It might be a room in your house,
or the alley where you play after school,
or a secret place no one else knows about.

Write about your special place.

- Where is it?
- What is it like?
- What do you do there?
- Why is it special?

Places in Stories

Sometimes adventures happen in a special place.
Sometimes they begin somewhere quite ordinary.
A story-writer needs to describe
the place where an adventure begins.
Let's follow Tom on one of his adventures.

Read and imagine

TOM CLIMBED DOWN FROM HIS TREEHOUSE. IT WAS TIME TO TAKE HIS DOG FOR A WALK.

THEY WALKED THROUGH THE TOWN AND OUT TOWARDS THE OPEN FIELDS.

THEY FOLLOWED THE FAMILIAR PATH THROUGH THE WOODS.

Where do you think they went next?

. . . the old cottage?

. . . the pool in the clearing?

. . the church and graveyard?

Or somewhere else?

Write a short but interesting description
of the place where Tom's adventure began.

4 Messages

School Trip

Poster
Each summer the children in some schools
get the chance to go on a trip
with some of the teachers.
Pretend you are going on a school trip.

Design a poster announcing the school trip.
Somewhere on the poster you need to write:

- the name of your class (for example P4 or Mrs. Bett's Class),
- the date of the trip (you decide),
- the place chosen for the trip (choose a real place you know or make one up),
- a sentence telling children who to go to for further information.

Make your poster look exciting so that lots of children will want to go on the trip.

Letter to Parents

Two weeks to go to school trip!

A letter is sent home to parents telling them all about the trip.

Write out the letter below filling in the missing information.

You decide the details.

```
             Your school's name and address

     _____


  Dear Parents,

  Plans for the school trip are now ready.

  Date and Time

  We shall leave school at_____on_____.

  Please make sure that your child is in the school playground

  by_____on that day.

  Please send a packed lunch.

  Going

  We will travel to_____by_____and

  hope to arrive at about_____.

  Returning

  We shall leave_____at_____

  on_____.  We hope to be back in

  school by_____.  Please come and collect

  your child then.

  We hope that everyone will have a really good time.

             Yours sincerely
```

Please bring . . .
Imagine that you are going on the school trip.
What would you need to get ready?

Write a list of everything you need to take with you.
Use the pictures and headings below to help you.

1. Clothing (Waterproof clothing and special gear for activities will be provided.)	*Remember* warm things cool things swim things	
2. Food	packed lunch for the journey snacks goodies	
3. Games, books and other things for the journey (You have to choose carefully as there isn't much room in your bag.)		
	N.B. Don't rely on the weather. Maybe the sun will shine all day. Maybe it will be cold and windy.	

Please Come to a Party!

Planning—Lists
Pretend you are going to have a party!
Imagine the kind of party you would most like to have.
Think about the friends you can invite.
Think about the games you can play.
Think about other things you can do.

Write what kind of party you would like. Say why.

Birthday

Halloween

Bonfire

Trampoline

Disco

Fancy Dress

Bar-B-Q

You need to plan your party well ahead of time.
Then everything will be ready on the day.
Lists are useful for planning ahead.

1. Who will come

Write a list of friends you want to invite.
List no more than ten including yourself.

2. Food and drink

Write a list of things to eat and drink.

3. Things to do

Write a list of games and activities.

4. What else will you do?

Make up a programme for your party.

Put in a time for each activity, like this:

3 pm	Friends arrive
3.30 pm	Treasure Hunt
4 pm	Tea

Planning—Invitations
Design a party invitation, reply slip and envelope.
Try to make the design say something about
the kind of party you are going to have.

The Invitation

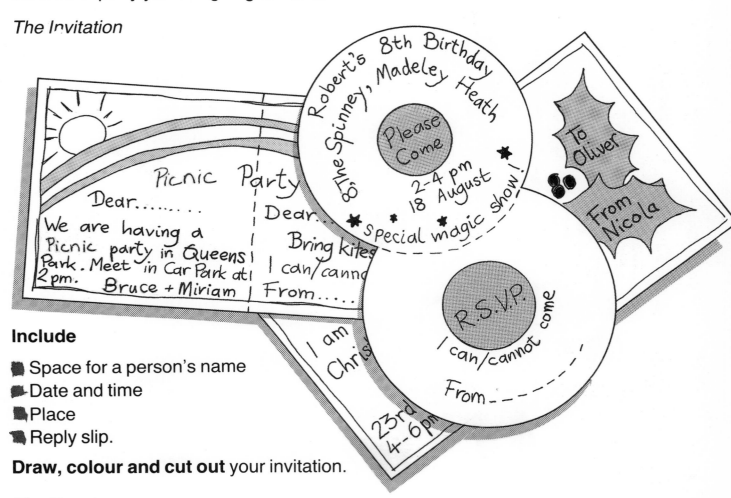

Picnic Party

Dear........

We are having a
Picnic party in Queens
Park. Meet in Car Park at
2pm.
Bruce + Miriam

Dear....
Bring kites
I can/cannot
From.....

I am
Chris....
23rd
4-6pm

Robert's 8th Birthday
8 The Spinney, Madeley Heath
Please Come
2-4 pm
18 August
★ ★ Special magic show! ★

R.S.V.P.
I can/cannot come
From - - - - -

To Oliver
From Nicola

Include

- Space for a person's name
- Date and time
- Place
- Reply slip.

Draw, colour and cut out your invitation.

The Envelope
Decorate an envelope to match your invitation.
Address it to one of your friends.
Like this

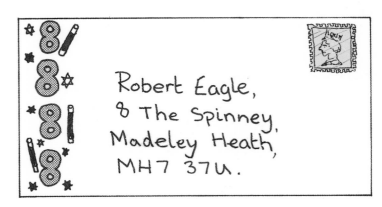

Robert Eagle,
8 The Spinney,
Madeley Heath,
MH7 37U.

39

Please Come to a Party!

Planning—Special Entertainment

In some towns you can book something special for a party.
Here are some of the special things we found in our local newspaper.
Which one would you choose for your party?

- clown
- video cartoon show
- magician
- puppet show
- disco-show (disc jockey + light show)
- Punch and Judy.

Or can you find or think of something different?

Write a letter to book a special act for your party.
The next page shows how to set out a letter.

How to lay out a letter
Use this page to help you write all your letters.
Think of a letter as having three sections.
The middle section is the longest. Here you give information
or reply to points made in a letter to you.

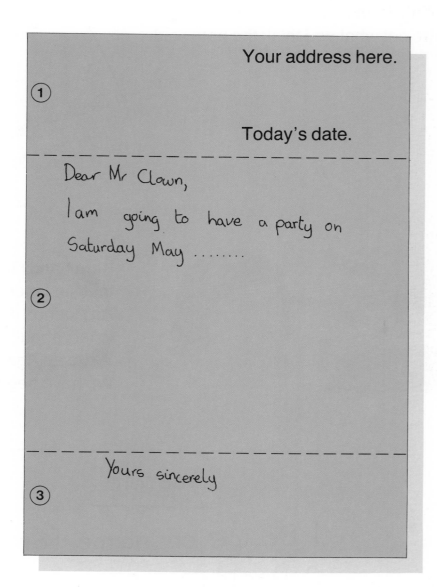

Your address here.

①

Today's date.

Dear Mr Clown,

I am going to have a party on Saturday May ....

②

Yours sincerely

③

If you know the person you can write

With best wishes

instead.

In your letter to book a special act you need to include:

- the date and time of your party,
- a request about the cost of the act,
- the number of children who will be there,
- your name clearly written.

Special Club

Note and Agenda
Karen and Greg have started a special club.
They wrote a note to some of their friends
inviting them to a first meeting.
Write out what you think the note said.

Karen and Greg need an **Agenda** for
their first meeting.
An Agenda is a list of things to do and
to talk about.
Write an Agenda for their first meeting.
We have begun one for you.

Agenda

1. Decide on name for club.
2. Decide on place to meet.
3. Vote for leader.

You don't have to use any of our ideas if you don't want to.

Badges and Membership Cards

Karen and Greg have decided on the sort of club they want.

They have chosen a leader.

Now they need badges and a membership card.

Badges

All the badges must show the club's special sign.

There is a different badge for the leader.

Design and make one badge for the leader and one for all the members.

Membership Cards

Club members also need membership cards.

These cards might show

- the member's name,
- the member's number,
- the secret password,
- what else?

You decide what will be written on the new club membership cards.

Then **design and make** a card for Karen, for Greg, or for yourself.

You can use our ideas or make up your own.

Codes

Karen and Greg can write messages to other members of the club in code.

The message they want to send is **MEET IN OUR SHED TONIGHT.**

Here are two ideas for codes.

1. Write the message backwards and change the spacing.
   The message becomes THGI NOTDE HS RU ONIT EEM.

2. Change each letter of the alphabet for another.
   You will all need a card like this to help you read and write messages.

A = O	H = V	O = C	V = J
B = P	I = W	P = D	W = K
C = Q	J = X	Q = E	X = L
D = R	K = Y	R = F	Y = M
E = S	L = Z	S = G	Z = N
F = T	M = A	T = H	
G = U	N = B	U = I	

The message becomes ASSH WB CIF GVSR HCBWUVH.

Decide on a message you would like to send to somebody.
Use one of the codes we suggest,
or make up a different one of your own.
Write your message in code.
See if a friend can work it out.

Record

By the end of term the children in the new club
have done all sorts of things.
They have met regularly.
They have been on several outings.

They have done one or two special things.
You decide what the children have done.
Write a record of events for the term.
You can use some of our ideas.
Or make up your own.

Record

September to December

Sat 21st Sept.
  1st club meeting in Billy's garage.

Sat 28th Sept
  2nd meeting
  Gave out cards and badges
  Chose Leader
  Decided next event

Fri 4th Oct
  Went swimming after school

Holidays

Notices

You often see notices in public places.

Some are warnings.

Some give information.

Look at the pictures of notices here.

Write the words which you think belong in each.

Think of another notice which you might see.

Draw a picture and put your notice in.

Posters—Explaining why

The posters below tell us to do something,
or not to do something.
But they don't tell us why.

Write a sentence or two to explain why for each poster.

Is there something else we ought to tell children about?
Design, draw and write a poster of your own.
Don't forget to **explain why** children should take notice.

Recipe

The pictures below show how to make sandwiches.

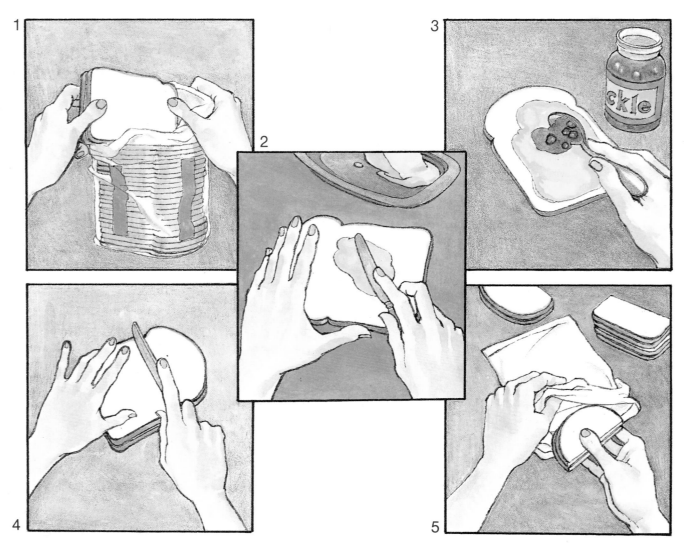

Write simple instructions for each picture like this:

1.   Take two slices of bread.

Draw your own set of pictures for something else
you would like to make for a picnic.
Choose something fairly simple.
Write short instructions for each picture.
You could muddle up your pictures
and see if a friend can sort them out.

Games

Think of a simple outdoor game that
you could explain to your friends.
It can be a well known game like Hide-and-Seek
or a game that you have made up.
Write instructions for the game so that
others will know how to play it.
We have begun one set of instructions to show you.

```
         HIDE AND SEEK

       An outdoor game for
         2 to 10 players


You need
Plenty of space
Places to hide


How to play
1.  One person hides his eyes and
counts slowly to 50.
2.  Everyone else runs away and
quietly finds a place to hide.
```

(Continue the instructions.)

Choose another simple game for a rainy day.
Write another set of instructions for it.

Holidays

Directions

Look at the picture of the fair on the opposite page.
Robin and Jane need directions.
Work out with a friend what you would say.

1. Jane wants to find her way
   from the ghost train to the ice cream stall.

   Write clear directions for Jane.

2. Robin wants to find his way from
   the Big Wheel to the gate.

   Write clear instructions for Robin.

Ghost
Train

GHOST   TRAIN

1. Start here

Helter-
Skelter

THE BIG SLIDE

Hoop-la

GRAY'S FAIR

IN   1OP   OUT

Dive bomber

DIVE BOMBER

Hot Dogs

HOT DOGS

Merry-go-round

ROUNDABOUT · ROUN

Big Wheel

CARNIVAL

BIG WHEEL

KEEP A
INSIDE

2. Start here

Shooting Gallery

Ice-cream

ICES

51

How to Use

Below are some things you might want to use on holiday.
Look at the first one.
It has a label with instructions.

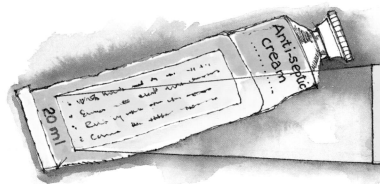

1. Wash hands and the cut or graze.
2. Squeeze out small amount of cream.
3. Rub gently into cut or graze.
4. Cover with plaster if necessary.

Write simple, numbered instructions for **one** of these two items.

Now **do the same** for **one** of these machines.

Think of something else that you might use on holiday.
Draw a picture of it and **write** instructions for using it.

6 Information

Swop-Shop

Pretend you are writing in to a Television Swop Programme.
You want to swop one of your toys or games for something else.

Write a short description of the toy you want to swop.
Write a short description of two or three things you would like instead.
We have done three swop cards below to show you how.

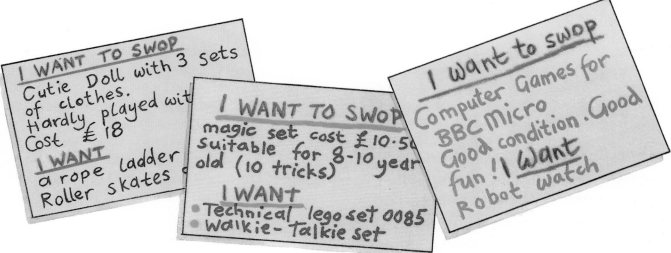

I WANT TO SWOP
Cutie Doll with 3 sets
of clothes.
Hardly played wit[h]
Cost £18
I WANT
a rope ladder
Roller skates

I WANT TO SWOP
magic set cost £10.5[0]
Suitable for 8-10 year
old (10 tricks)
I WANT
• Technical lego set 0085
• Walkie-Talkie set

I want to swop
Computer Games for
BBC Micro
Good condition. Good
fun! I Want
Robot watch

For Sale Ad

If you do not manage to swop it, you can try to sell
your unwanted toy or game in the local newspaper.
Write your ad so that other children will be interested.
Include your name and phone number or address.
Like this

For Sale   £45
Super BMX bike
Black with lots of stickers
Excellent condition
Suit 8-10 year old
Reason for sale: too small now
Phone: Paul Richards 021-427-4130

Advertising ME!

Pretend you have been captured
by an alien from outer space.
He is going to sell you to a time lord
who wants a child like you to live in his
space city.
First you must be advertised on their
computer system.

What will the advert say about you?
Write a good description of yourself.
Use the headings below to help you or
make up other headings if you want.
Remember to write **good** things about yourself
so that time lords will want to buy you!

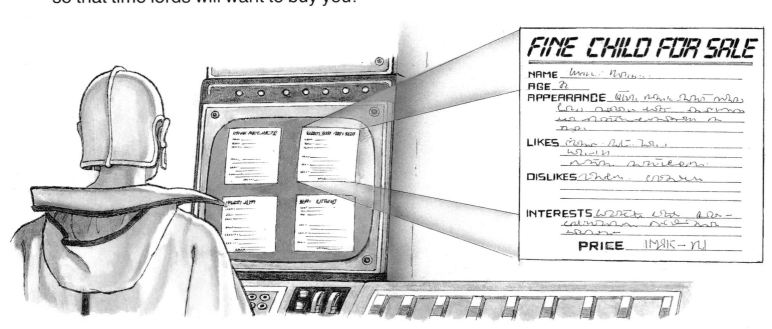

Scene of the Crime

Today Errol stayed late at school for the computer club.
When he arrived home he saw that someone had broken
into the shed and stolen his bike.
This is what he saw. Are there any clues?

Later Errol's mother phoned the police.
They asked Errol to describe exactly what he saw —
he was the first person at the scene of the crime.

Write a short statement for the police.
Describe exactly what Errol noticed.

Police Wanted

Errol remembered something more that might help the police.
Two weeks ago he spotted two big boys coming out of his gate.
He saw one of them quite clearly.
He told the police and they asked for a detailed description
of the boy Errol saw.
From the details he gave they were able to make up a poster.

Choose someone in your class.
Write and draw a Police Wanted Notice,
like the one on the next page.
Write a few facts about the person you have chosen.
Can the rest of the class guess who it is?

POLICE WANTED

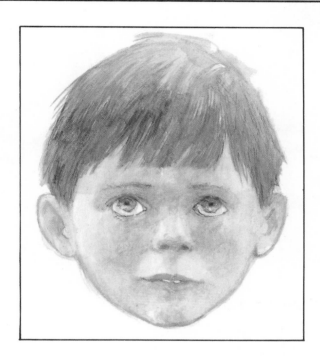

Age:	8½ years
Height:	1 metre 40 cm
Build:	Skinny
Hair:	Light mousy. Thick & straight
Eyes:	Round and pale blue
Nose:	Flat and blunt
Mouth:	Wide (usually talking)
Special Features:	Two big front teeth
Last seen wearing:	Jeans, check shirt, red anorak, cap covered in badges.

Imagine your bike has been stolen.
The police want an exact description of it.
This is different from the advert that you wrote before.
Your description must be really accurate.
The more details you give, the more chance the police
have of finding your bike.

Write an exact, detailed description of your bike.
(You can describe your own bike or make up a description.)
Use the list below to help you think of all the details.

Make	Scratches or rust patches
Colour	Faulty parts
Condition	Stickers
Age	Special points
Extras	

Zoo Animals

Cathy is at the zoo.
Her class are doing a project about zoo animals.
Cathy is reading the notice by the pool of the
Blackfooted Penguins.
Look at the notice.

BLACKFOOTED PENGUINS

Live in the warm coastal regions of South Africa.

They are flightless.
They use their flippers to propel themselves through the water.

Diet consists of fish, squid and shellfish.

Write what Cathy should put in her notes, under these headings:

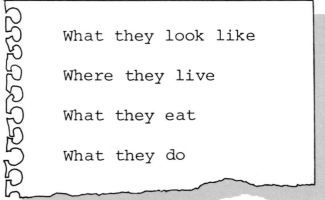

What they look like

Where they live

What they eat

What they do

Write a short notice about another zoo animal.
You may need to read about your animal in a book first.

Write only a few important facts about your animal.

Zoo Animals

Monkey
Lion
Owl
Sea Lion
Penguin
Piranha
Camel
Eel
Tortoise
Zebra
Vulture

Cathy needs some help with her project.
There are so many animals and birds to write about.
She wants to divide her project book into sections
so that it is easier for other pupils to read.
Can you think of three different sections?
Cathy wants to include all the animals and birds shown on this page.

Write three headings for your three groups of animals.
Under each heading list the animals that belong to each group.

Bar Charts

Cathy's teacher asked the class about their favourite zoo animals.
They decided to make a bar chart showing the answers they gave.
This is what it looked like.

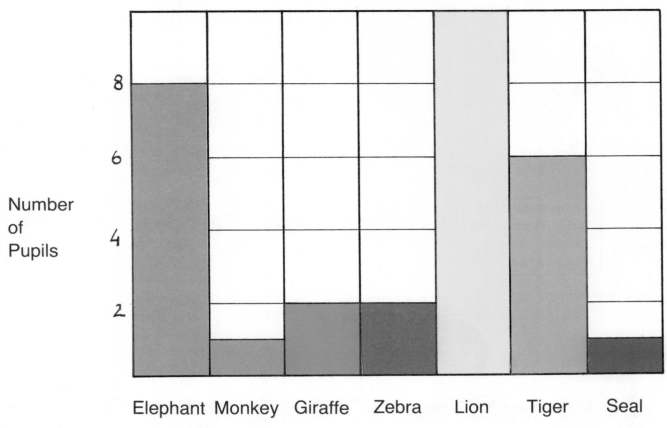

Carry out a survey in your class.
It can be a survey of favourite zoo animals **or** favourite pets.

Do it like this.
1. **Make** a tally chart, like Cathy's.
2. **Note** how many there are in the biggest list.
3. **Work out** the size of your bar chart.
4. **Draw, colour and write out** your bar chart on a large sheet of paper.

Children's Newsbeat

Here are today's news headlines.

A DANGEROUS TIGER ESCAPED TODAY FROM A MIDLANDS SAFARI PARK.
MORE LATER.

TEACHERS ALL OVER THE COUNTRY BEGAN A THREE DAY STRIKE TODAY.

CHILDREN FROM ONE PRIMARY SCHOOL HAVE RAISED £1000 FOR OUR FAMINE APPEAL.
HOW DID THEY DO IT?
MORE LATER.

AND FINALLY A BRITISH SCHOOLGIRL HAS WON A VERY SPECIAL AWARD.

Choose **one** of the stories on Children's Newsbeat.
Write the full story that the announcer reads after the headlines.
Pretend that you are a TV news reader.
Read the news story that you have written to some of your friends.

The Jumping Bus

Imagine you work for a newspaper.
You have been sent to take some photos of a new swing bridge.
To your amazement this is what you see!

What a scoop!
You rush back to the newspaper office with your photos.

Write a newspaper report to go with the pictures.
Add a headline.
Include the best picture (you draw it).

P.S. This is a true story.

Headlines

Here are some newspaper headlines.
Which story sounds most interesting?

Advertiser

Panda born in Zoo

Morning Sun

School pop group have No.1. hit

DAILY NEWS

Scientists discover life on distant planet

Evening Star

Seaside rescue

Choose **one** story headline.
Imagine what happened.

Write a short newspaper report to go with the headline.
Or make up a different headline of your own and write the story.